DISCARD

Arkansas

Arkansas
Matt Bradley

BRADLEY PUBLISHING

To my wife, Susan, and my mother,
Mildred Bradley, for giving me the
greatest gift of all—love.

Published by Bradley Publishing

Copyright © 1996 by Matt Bradley

Inquiries should be addressed to
Bradley Publishing
15 Butterfield Lane
Little Rock, Arkansas 72212
Phone 501 224-0692
Fax 501 224-0762

99 98 97 96   4 3 2 1

Library of Congress Catalogue Card Number: 96-83583

ISBN 0-940716-02-X   Regular Edition
ISBN 0-940716-03-8   Limited Gift Edition

Printed and bound in Korea

Photography workshop group at the Hawksbill Crag,
Ozark National Forest; (preceding pages) Highway 374
near Jasper

Contents

Acknowledgments

ALLTEL

With pride and gratitude I salute the employees of ALLTEL
for their commitment to this book and to Arkansas.

Special thanks to the following organizations and companies
whose support helped make this first edition a reality:

Arkansas Department of Parks and Tourism

Arkansas Environmental Federation

Arkansas Industrial Development Commission

Department of Arkansas Heritage

Entergy

First Commercial Bank

Little Rock Convention and Visitors Bureau

The Nature Conservancy

Orbit Valve Company

Stephens Inc.

Preface

Twenty years have slipped by since my first book on Arkansas.

During that time, my camera has led me to some pretty incredible places, from Norway to Bali, the Caribbean to Alaska. While looking through a lens, I've dangled from the top of a sailboat mast in the Virgin Islands, backed into a cactus in the Sonoran Desert and camped in -30 degree temperature in the Canadian Arctic.

For all these years, no matter where my travels have taken me, I always look forward to coming back home to Arkansas.

There is a certain quality to life here which I savor and haven't found anywhere else—a combination of the varied landscape and easy-going attitude of the people. The feelings that I have for Arkansas are strictly positive, deeply personal and hard to express with words.

I hope the photographs that follow communicate not only what I have seen while behind the camera but also what I have felt.

They are truly pictures taken from the heart.

Shannon Butler at Riverfest, Little Rock

A Gentle Beauty

River, forest, mountain, prairie. The land that is Arkansas defies quick definition.

Distinct geographic regions possess a common beauty altered by the changing seasons—a beauty that soothes more often than astounds, a beauty that whispers rather than shouts.

Join me and take a close look at the land and people of the Natural State.

Ouachita Mountains, Montgomery County

As we travel across this state in any direction there is one certainty: the form, color and texture of the landscape will change.

Harvesting soybeans on the Grand Prairie

Cossatot River State Park-Natural Area

Morning fog, Ozark Mountains

American Lotus, Felsenthal National Wildlife Refuge

Waterskier on the Arkansas River, Little Rock

Maple trees, Highway 7 Scenic Byway

"As one of nature's storytellers, I always feel humble when I try to explain things—like these six-hundred-year-old cypress trees.

"Just think, they were already good-sized trees when the first Europeans arrived in Arkansas. They've survived lightning strikes, tornados, floods, drought and ice storms, and they're still clinging to life.

"Nature just never gives up."

Neil Curry, naturalist
Pinnacle Mountain State Park

Kingfisher Trail, Pinnacle Mountain State Park

Lake Enterprise, near Wilmot

"Contrary to popular opinion, moisture is not the most important factor in determining fall color. Neither is frost.

"It's the change of seasons—the cool, cloudless nights and shorter days—that kills chlorophyll in the leaves, leaving a yellow pigment that was always there. Sugars made during photosynthesis are changed into red pigment.

"The mixture of these reds and yellows produces the range of colors that gives us our fall beauty."

Don Culwell, Professor of Biology
University of Central Arkansas

Maple tree details, Ouachita National Forest

Haw Creek, near Pelsor

Fall leaves on a pond in Allsopp Park, Little Rock

Maple trees in the Ozark National Forest;
(facing page) eastern end of Lake Ouachita

Bracket fungi along the Lost Valley Trail,
Buffalo National River

At least once during the course of every photography workshop I find myself telling my students, "Be careful where you walk; you might be stepping on a picture."

Christmas ferns, St. Francis National Forest

One November evening while driving across the Delta, one of those unforgettable silver moons crept above the horizon.

With twilight fading to darkness, I found the silhouette of a pecan tree to place against the moon. Working quickly to set up tripod and camera, I noticed my breath hanging in the frosty air and my fingers starting to stiffen.

Winter could not be far away.

Pecan tree near Lake Chicot;
(facing page) Little Maumelle River

Everyone always thinks of fall as Arkansas's
premier color season. Well, I for one, would like
to nominate spring.

Bluets, Little Rock (left); young red oak leaves, Richland Creek Wilderness (right)

Hillside mixture of pine and hardwood, western Pulaski County

Spiderworts on the summit of Tall Peak,
Ouachita National Forest

Ozark Mountains in April

"Wildflowers provide the low vegetation we need for safety and erosion control, and they require very little maintenance. So, over the past several years we've changed our mowing habits in many areas to allow Mother Nature to take her course.

"We consider the ecology of the roadsides as well as the aesthetics and are becoming better stewards of the land."

Wendy Welch, biologist
Arkansas Highway and
Transportation Department

Narrow-leaved sunflowers along U.S. Highway 371, near Magnolia

As a photographer, I never tire of watching the magical play of light on water, ever changing to the whims of nature.

A breath of wind gives a lake fresh texture; riverbed boulders alter a current's character.

A gentle beauty, the only constant.

Lake Maumelle

River detail, Cossatot River State Park-Natural Area

Lake Ouachita

Sunrise, Beaver Lake

Cattails, west of Magnolia

A Sense of Community

"When I first came to Searcy in July of '91 for a temporary job, I thought I would be here only one month.

"I started hearing about the Holiday of Lights my second day in town. The longer I stayed the more I heard, so I decided to get involved. I couldn't believe how well the city—the entire community—worked together. You could just feel the pride.

"My husband and I decided this was the kind of place we wanted our family to grow up in. We moved here in December."

Tracy Tidwell, Searcy

Christmas Holiday of Lights, White County Courthouse Square, Searcy

"There's something perfect about the geographical setting of Little Rock, especially as seen from the air—the sense of the hills to the west with the river cranking down the middle. You have trees, highways and buildings that look just the way they should.

"It's like the kind of idealized American city that you might design for a movie set or a model train layout. Big enough to be called a city, but small enough to be comprehended all at once."

Gene Lyons, writer
Little Rock

Downtown Little Rock

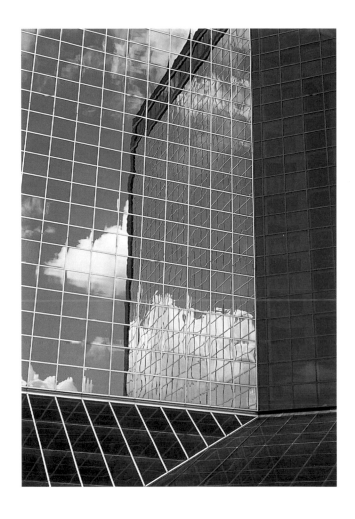

Arkansas's first state capitol, used from 1836 to 1911, now known as the Old State House (left); the Excelsior Hotel, Little Rock (right)

Williams Magnet School fifth graders on the grand stairs leading to the Senate Chamber, State Capitol

"Allsopp Park has always been one of my favorite places. When I was just a boy, I would find any excuse to go there. Now, forty years later, it's still just like it was back then.

"Right in the heart of Little Rock is this natural, beautiful place for me to enjoy with my kids and, hopefully someday, my grandchildren."

Barry Travis, Executive Director
Little Rock Convention and
Visitors Bureau

Allsopp Park hiking trail, Little Rock

"No matter what is being bought or sold, good relationships provide the foundation for good business."

Warren Stephens, CEO
Stephens Inc.

Sales and trading floor, Stephens Inc. (facing page):
Farmers' Market, Little Rock

"Sure, it still amazes me when I think that customers in Yakota, Japan, withdraw cash from an ATM and *we* process the transaction instantaneously here in Little Rock.

"With today's communications network, it just doesn't matter anymore where the computer is located, so we manage information from all over the world. The Command Center is where we watch it all happen.

"People say it's a lot like *Star Wars*. It is, except it's real."

Ed Stevens, Vice President
ALLTEL Information Services

Command Center at ALLTEL Information Services, Little Rock

Jan's Barber Shop, Marshall

"There's no telling who you'll find sitting on our porch. We've had visitors from all over the world.

"Lots of times they just chat; sometimes they play a little music. But there are always lots of stories being told."

Don Mellon, Mountain View

Mellon's Country Store, Mountain View

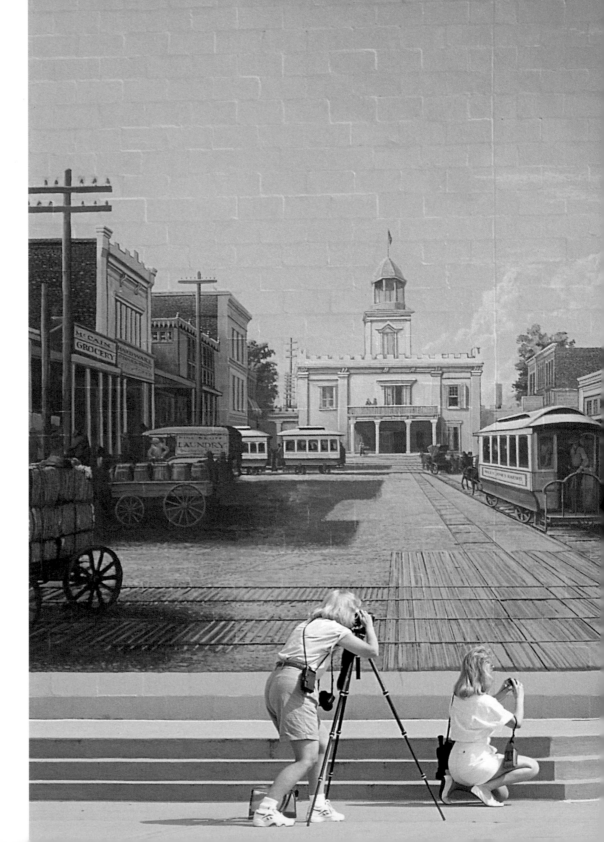

Memories come flooding back when I think of growing up in Pine Bluff: the time I first learned to ride a bicycle, first fell in love (in the sixth grade) and first attempted to take meaningful photographs—of my high school classmates for the yearbook.

At our thirty-year class reunion, it seemed ironic to find myself once again behind the camera with some of the same high school friends in front of the lens.

A photographic career had come full circle.

A group from the class of '65 in front of Robert Dafford's mural depicting Pine Bluff's main street in 1888

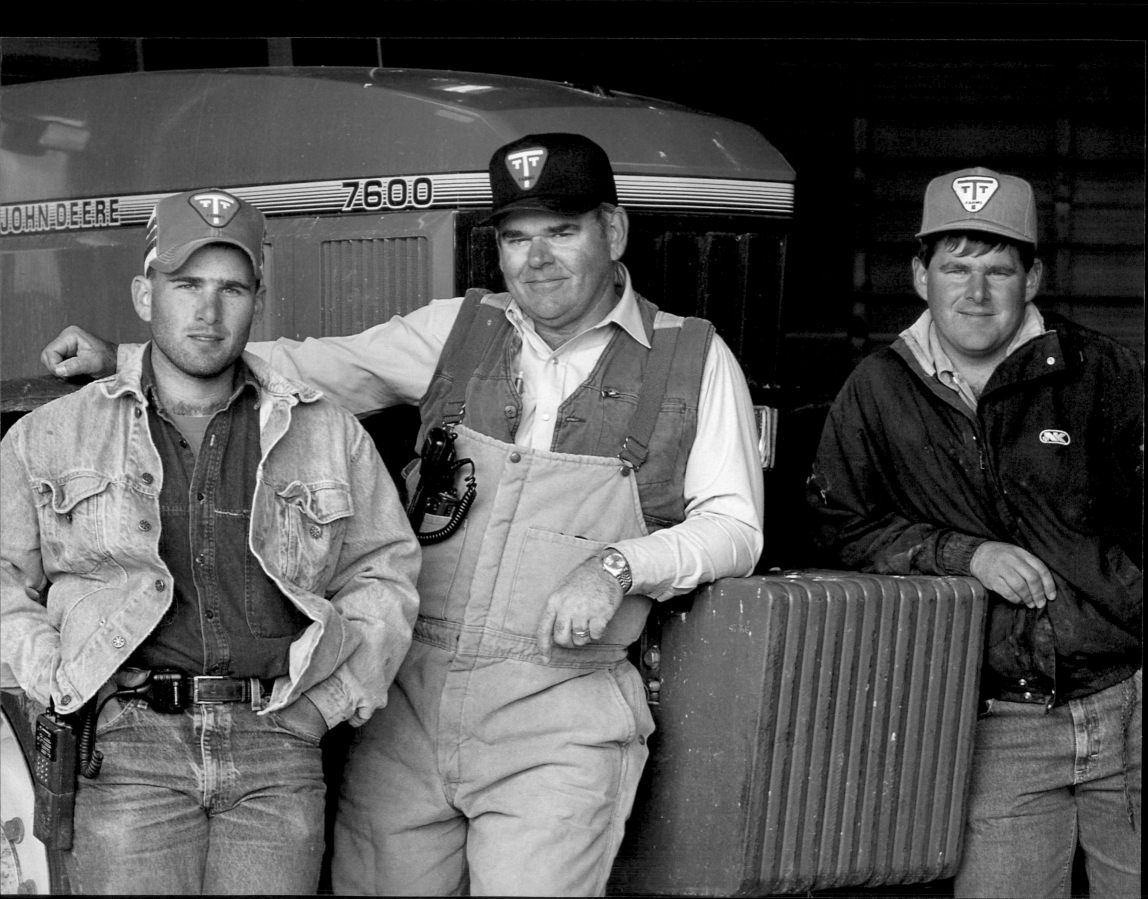

"Our roots are deep in this land.

"I'm the fourth generation of my family to farm this place. Ever since we had two boys it's been a dream of mine. working side-by-side with my sons.

"I've changed both their diapers on tractors—I'd pack my sandwich. take their bottles and we'd spend the day together. To my knowledge. they've never wanted to do anything else.

"My dream has come true."

John Ed Tarkington. Triple T Farms
Almyra

*John Ed Tarkington with sons, Will and Sam, 1977;
(facing page) Tarkington men, 1995*

"The mail comes around noon, but folks usually get here early—and it's gossip time."

Bridget Henson, clerk
Gilbert General Store

Front of old post office, Gilbert General Store

Bunch's Store, Kingston

"Bud Walton Arena has the most electric atmosphere in college basketball today.

"When the band starts to play and that big flag comes out of the south tunnel with the team running behind—well, any Razorback fan is going to get goose bumps."

Rick Schaeffer, Director
University of Arkansas Sports Information

Bud Walton Arena, University of Arkansas, Fayetteville

*Magnolia Blossom Festival featuring the World Championship
Steak Cookoff and talent show, Magnolia*

"When I need a break, I'm off to a festival. Each one is a special little Arkansas treasure."

Joe David Rice, Tourism Director
Arkansas Department of
Parks and Tourism

Toad races during "Toad Suck Daze," Conway

"Quartz, Quiltz and Craftz" Festival, Mt. Ida

"Hope watermelons have a warm spot in my heart since they were largely responsible for my meeting Bill.

"One afternoon as I was walking through the student lounge at Yale Law School, I heard this booming voice exclaim, 'And not only that, we have the largest watermelons in the world!' Well, I was certainly curious about a man who could be so enthusiastic about watermelons.

"And the rest, as they say, is history."

Hillary Rodham Clinton
First Lady

Hope watermelon

Many of our festivals and special events give a quick glimpse into the past.

I arrived early to photograph Fort Smith's rodeo parade (far right), and that's how I happened to meet Charles Campbell. A third generation rancher from nearby Scullyville, Oklahoma, he peeled back the years from my photo composition looking down Garrison Avenue.

"You see that first stoplight up there?" he asked. "They used to call that Texas Corner. And just across the river was the largest horse and mule trading market in this part of the country—right on the border of Indian Territory."

Crosscut saw competition, Bradley County Pink Tomato Festival; (facing page) Rodeo parade, Fort Smith

I started playing the guitar when I was ten," Johnny Billington (near right) told me during Helena's King Biscuit Blues Festival.

"Two years later I started playing juke joints. That was in the 50s; I made twenty dollars a night while my parents were making eighteen dollars a week."

After a nineteen-year stint in Chicago as a professional musician and mechanic, he now teaches children about music, the blues and something more.

"I tell my kids: you go through life just bouncing around without a plan—doin' this, doin' that. Pretty soon you're old and you ain't done nothing.

"The Bible says you got to stay on the road if you want to get to the Kingdom. That's what I try to teach kids today."

Johnny Billington, Helena

Joe Louis Walker and the Bosstalkers during the King Biscuit Blues Festival, Helena

Special Places, Interesting People

"I don't talk much about the cave before taking a group to see it for the first time. I just wait for the elevator door to open and watch their jaws drop as they look out over that vast, wonderful room.

"There is no way words can prepare them for that moment."

John David McFarland, geologist
Arkansas Geological Commission

Along the Dripstone Trail, Blanchard Springs Cavern

I have long been fascinated with Arkansas's craftsmen. Not only are their products visually appealing, but frequently the creator is as interesting as the craft.

Such is the case with Leon Niehues (right). Soft spoken and articulate, Leon related how jobs were scarce when he and his wife, Sharon, first came to the Ozarks in the mid-70s.

Anxious for ways to supplement their income, Leon found a county extension service booklet on basketmaking. With little to lose and everything to gain, Leon and Sharon mutually agreed to take the plunge and devote their energies to this new endeavor.

Leon looked me straight in the eyes and said, "There was no way I was going to fail."

Leon Niehues in his studio outside of Pettigrew

*Handmade brooms by Judy and Jerry Lovenstein,
Mountain View*

"Wood won't do just anything you want it to. Because of its grain, it has capabilities and limitations built into it.

"Some carvers are successful by using basic tools and letting the wood do most of the talking. But when we were carving, we used more sophisticated tools and tried to push the wood to its limits, even going against the grain to get added fluffiness and fragile detail.

"By the time up to twelve layers of paint were added, the wood would almost be silent. We've had lots of people ask us if our birds were stuffed. We'd say no, they were made of wood, and we'd smile. That was just what we wanted to hear."

Gerry Chisholm, artist
Mountain View

Miniature carving by Nona Warren Teague, Mountain View (above); goldfinch by Sheri and Gerry Chisholm (right)

72

Goldeneye by Carolyn and Jim Cushing, Mountain View

William McNamara in Dug Hollow, Newton County

Though different in many ways, William McNamara and Henri Linton share a common passion—depicting the beauty of the Arkansas landscape on canvas.

McNamara (far left) is a widely acknowledged master of portraying the Ozarks, especially the Buffalo River country, with watercolors. Frequently, the outdoors serves as his studio.

Henri Linton (near left), chairman of the Art Department at the University of Arkansas at Pine Bluff, has developed a national following for his compositions of the Delta as seen from an aerial perspective.

Unlike McNamara, Linton seldom paints directly from nature.

"My paintings are the results of observation, experience and memory," he says. "The landscapes represent no definite place, yet they are everywhere you go."

Henri Linton in his studio, Pine Bluff

"There seems to be something lofty and uplifting in seeking religious contemplation, so I've always felt something tall was fitting for a religious structure. Whatever we're searching for, it seems to be 'up there.'

"For me, the strongest indication we have of a higher power can be felt in nature. When I can, I always try to incorporate the beauty of nature into the building itself and make the outside part of the inner space."

Fay Jones, architect
Fayetteville

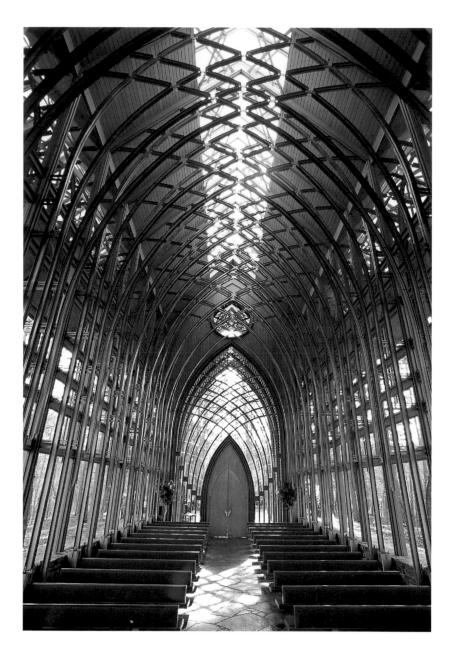

Mildred B. Cooper Memorial Chapel designed by Fay Jones, Bella Vista

76

Beechwood Baptist Church, Ponca

Central Avenue, Hot Springs

I seem to learn something more about the remarkable geology of Hot Springs with each visit. Its history is the story of its water, 850,000 gallons per day of it gushing from 47 outlets on the side of a mountain.

Of those who enjoy it, whether bathing or drinking, few realize that this water, bubbling out of the ground at 143 degrees Fahrenheit, has been determined to be 4,000 years old.

"Hot Water Cascade," Hot Springs National Park

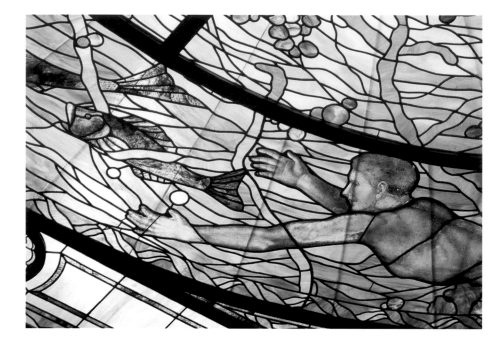

If anyone knows Hot Springs history, it's national park ranger Toni Cooper (above) who has been directing tours since 1981.

"What we know today as Bathhouse Row," she says, "is actually the third generation of structures. First there were just canvas tents, then wooden buildings and now these wonderful old structures of marble, tile and stained glass.

"In its heyday in the mid-1940s, Bathhouse Row had a million bathers a year."

Toni Cooper (above); stained glass skylight and fountain, Fordyce Bath House (right)

Bathhouse Row, Hot Springs National Park

Arkansas's entrepreneurs come in all shapes and sizes, each with an interesting story to tell.

When I first photographed Joan Johnson back in 1977 (above), she and husband, Bruce, were part of the back-to-the-land movement. They had built their own house, grown a big garden and birthed their two children at home.

Recently, I had the chance to photograph them again (near right) and discovered their lives had changed. While pursuing a carpentry career, Bruce had discovered an untapped market for hardwood lumber. Now their business, White River Hardwoods, ships internationally and grosses well over six million dollars a year.

Joan Johnson 1977 (above); Bruce and Joan Johnson in a White River Hardwoods warehouse, Fayetteville (right)

If anyone knows "which came first," it would be Don Tyson (left) who has grown the poultry processing business started by his father into the nation's largest, serving a world-wide market.

Senior Chairman Don Tyson, Tyson Foods, Inc., Springdale

"To a large extent, Arkansas *is* a forest. We can keep it that way forever if we work together."

John T. Shannon, State Forester
Arkansas Forestry Commission

Ouachita National Forest

It's an other-worldly experience, standing in the middle of an oil refinery. Gleaming towers rise up from miles of winding pipes and conduit. Vents hiss billowing clouds of steam.

But things looked different in 1921, ninety-three-year-old Ruben Dees (above) told me.

"You could stand on the top of Snow Hill and it was a pretty good sight," he related. "More derricks than you could count, many of them a'gushin. There was oil everywhere—on the ground, in the grass, in the trees and in the air. When I'd come home—and in those days home was a tent—well, it would be dripping oil too."

Ruben Dees (above); wooden derrick replica at the Arkansas Oil and Brine Museum, Smackover (right)

Cross Refinery, Smackover

"The imprint of a deer's hoof is a negative in wet sand. Clear, distinct and observable. Our industrial and agricultural tracks are clear and discernible as well.

"Wind or rising water quickly erases the deer sign, but man must work to erase the imprint he leaves on the landscape. As citizens, this is a task we all must know about and work to complete."

Randy Wilbourn, Chairman
Arkansas Pollution Control and
Ecology Commission

Low-emission, electric arc furnace used to melt recycled scrap metal, Nucor Yamato Steel Company, Blytheville; (facing page) artificial marsh, built by Albemarle Corporation to naturally treat waste water, Magnolia

Boxley Valley, Newton County

"Newton County is a landscape of extremes. Start paddling down the Buffalo River and you'll find the highest waterfall and the highest cliff face in mid-America before you've gone ten miles.

"But it's the lesser known—the hidden places—I find the most rewarding. That little crease of a canyon that gives you a special sense of discovery, the feeling that no one else has been here before.

"That's the kind of place where you can find your inner self."

Mike Mills, Buffalo Outdoor Center, Ponca

Indian Creek, Buffalo National River

Spring regatta, Lake Maumelle

"We're learning about the original Arkansans, you might say.

"The site we're excavating at Parkin was established around A.D. 1000. We know for sure that it was still occupied when the expedition of Hernando de Soto came through in 1541.

"Head vases that have been found show us what these people actually looked like—how they shaved their heads, pierced their ears and cut designs in their faces to leave patterned scars.

"We think these vases may be portraits of enemies killed in battle, kept as trophies by the victor."

Dr. Jeff Mitchem, Station Archeologist
Parkin Archeological State Park

Effigy or "head" vase, Hampson Museum State Park;
(facing page) Parkin Archeological State Park

Flying over the Grand Prairie in September with harvest season in full swing below, it's hard for me to imagine that this area was once judged unsuitable for agriculture.

It wasn't until the early 1900s that it was determined that the same hardpan of clay limiting the growth of trees was perfect for the production of rice.

Combines harvesting rice on the Grand Prairie

Offering a distinct contrast to the flat prairie, Crowley's Ridge rises an average of two hundred feet above the eastern Arkansas Delta. Its foundation was formed millions of years ago by marine sediments from the Gulf of Mexico. This material was then eroded during a time when the Mississippi River flowed on the west side and the Ohio on the east side, leaving only a narrow spine of land in between.

Later, this ridge was further covered by a thick layer of rich, windblown soil known as "loess."

A sprig of purple phlox amidst a luxuriant growth of May apples, Village Creek State Park on Crowley's Ridge

"The first bunch that'll come in are usually young 'uns—immatures. They've only made one trip down the flyway and don't know enough to be cautious.

"The old ones follow, first maybe one hundred or so, then three hundred, one thousand and then ten thousand. Next thing you know, you've got a tornado of wings wheeling over your head."

Hoot Gibson, hunting guide
Almyra

*Hoot Gibson; (facing page) blue and snow geese over a
Grand Prairie rice field*

Mike and Chris Codling's version of the American dream has a face only a mother could love with an attitude to match.

Standing eight feet tall and weighing over three hundred pounds, Joe, the Codlings' senior ostrich, rushed at me spitting and hissing whenever I tried to ease close enough for a picture. When he kicked the fence separating us, the whole enclosure shuddered.

"The males can be a little aggressive," Chris shrugged, "especially when they're with a hen. But we see ostrich farming as the wave of the future. The birds have red meat with a beef-like taste, low in fat and cholesterol.

"It offers a way for people to get into farming that doesn't require a huge initial investment."

Joe, Sunrise Ostrich Ranch, Magnolia

"Life on a dairy farm has its ups and downs. But it's given all our kids a sense of responsibility and taught them how to work with their hands and their minds.

"I can't imagine living anywhere else."

Terry Riddle, dairy farmer
Damascus

Terry, Sandra and seven-year-old Julie Riddle with an overly hungry calf (left); Julie with friends in the "swimming pool" (above)

"My great-grandfather had a gin in Lepanto in the 20s; my grandfather operated gins for over sixty years. I just like the structures— they're part of the landscape around here.

"When Dell and I decided to build a house, I traveled around northeast Arkansas for a year taking pictures of old gins. We wanted a home that would blend in with other buildings in the area.

"We both like things that are a little different —that make people think."

Henry Grady "Tri" Watkins III, Lepanto

Tri and Dell Watkins with Gus, in front of their home near Lepanto; (facing page) cotton pickers, near Lepanto

"Traveling the Great River Road is like going back in time."

Claude Jenkins, Chairman
Mississippi River Parkway Commission

Mississippi River Bridge, Helena

The Mississippi Queen *and* Delta Queen, *near Helena*

You can explore the Ouachita Mountains by hiking trails or driving the back roads, but to really grasp their scale and remoteness, the exploring is best done by air.

I remember one fall flight in particular; the colors became more spectacular and the terrain more rugged the further west we flew.

Looking east near the Caney Creek Wilderness, Ouachita Mountains

On another photo mission in early summer we circled Lake Ouachita, crown jewel in Arkansas's treasury of lakes.

Just add a few palm trees, I thought while admiring the scene below, and you've got the Caribbean islands.

Lake Ouachita

Ansata Halim Shah

"Our Arabians have given us a global life.

"We've sold horses to state stud farms in Europe, business people in Australia and breeders in South America. The King of Morocco, the ruling Sheikh of Qatar and the royal family of Jordan are among our customers.

"Our horses have been a catalyst and a bridge—to other cultures, other climes, and to wonderful people from all walks of life."

Judith Forbis, Mena

Judith Forbis at "Ansata," her Egyptian-Arabian horse-breeding farm near Mena

Buffalo National River, as seen from the Goat Trail

"Rivers are always moving, always changing. They are more a force of nature than something that can be owned.

"You can't build a fence around a river. That's why people are drawn to them."

Jane Jones, Director
Arkansas Natural and Scenic
Rivers Commission

White River at sunrise

Kayakers Andy Hicks (left) and Nathan Kline, Cossatot River State Park-Natural Area

Nathan Kline negotiating a drop at Cossatot Falls

Murray Lock and Dam #7 on the Arkansas River, Little Rock

"I don't consider taking people fishing work. It's a way to make a living but not a job.

"Now, if I had to work hard enough to be able to afford two hundred float trips a year—that's a job."

Hank Wilson, guide
Gaston's White River Resort

Brown trout and Hank Wilson; (facing page) float fishermen at sunrise, White River

Steve Flanigan, Little Missouri River

Sheila Gass and Frank Barton, Buffalo National River

River, forest, mountain or prairie—how does one describe Arkansas? After a twenty-year career as a professional observer, I'm still not sure.

There is one thing I am sure of, and that's the feeling I get everytime I say that Arkansas is my home. . . .

Pride.

On the Goat Trail, Buffalo National River;
(facing page) Lake Enterprise, Wilmot

Bella Vista Village **4**
Pea Ridge Nat'l Mil. Pk.
Mammoth Spring
Bentonville
Eureka Springs
Berryville
BEAVER LAKE
Beaver Lake S.P.
Bull Shoals
Lakeview
NORFORK LAKE
Mammoth Spring S.P.
62
Piggott
Siloam Springs
Rogers
1
Withrow Springs S.P.
Harrison
Bull Shoals S.P.
Mountain Home
Salem
Ash Flat
Hardy
Pocahontas
7
Springdale
412
412
Yellville
Calico Rock
167
Walnut Ridge
Old Davidsonville S.P.
Crowley's Ridge S.P.
Paragould
Huntsville
Kingston
Prairie Grove S.P.
Fayetteville
Boxley
Ponca
Lost Valley
Jasper
3
14
Gilbert
Marshall
29
Buffalo Point
2
Ozark Folk Center S.P.
Lake Charles S.P.
Powhatan Courthouse S.P.
Evening Shade
63
Lake Frierson S.P.
Blytheville
Manila
Herman Davis Hist. Mon
55
Prairie Grove
23
26
Mountain View
22
Batestville
67
Jonesboro
Osceola
Lepanto
11
Hampson Museum
Wilson
Winslow
Devil's Den S.P.
12
Pelsor
Fairfield Bay
Greers Ferry
Jacksonport S.P.
Newport
Lake Poinsett S.P.
Lake Ft. Smith S.P.
7
Clinton
GREERS FERRY LAKE
167
Harrisburg
63
Van Buren
40
Alma
Clarksville
Ozark
Altus
Russellville
65
Heber Springs
Bald Knob
24
Parkin
Parkin Arch. S.P.
55
Fort Smith
540
LAKE DARDANELLE
Lake Dardanelle S.P.
40
67
167
Searcy
Village Creek S.P.
28
40
West Memphis
Ft. Smith Nat'l. Historic Site
Paris
Booneville
Mt. Nebo S.P.
Dardanelle
Morrilton
Conway
Woolly Hollow S.P.
67
167
Prairie County Museum
Forrest City
79
71
BLUE MTN. L.
Danville
21
Ola
Petit Jean S.P.
LAKE CONWAY
Brinkley
Marianna
27
NIMROD L.
7
Maumelle
North Little Rock
L. MAUMELLE
Pinnacle Mtn. S.P.
18
25
Jacksonville
40
Hazen
49
Queen Wilhelmina S.P.
"Y" City
14
Hot Springs Village
Lonoke
Louisiana Purchase Hist. Mon.
Helena
17
Lake Ouachita S.P.
Little Rock
430
Plant. Agri. Museum
Scott
West Helena
Mena
OUACHITA
LAKE OUACHITA
Hot Springs
Lake Catherine S.P.
630
Benton
Toltec Mounds Arch. S.P.
9
1
Cossatot River S.P.
6
Mount Ida
H.S. Nat'l. Pk.
LAKE HAMILTON
13
30
England
Stuttgart
DeWitt
19
Kirby
Glenwood
DeGRAY LAKE
Malvern
Jenkins' Ferry Battleground Hist. Mon.
Sheridan
65
Almyra
DIERKS L.
Daisy S.P.
DeGray Lake Resort S.P.
Pine Bluff
165
Ark. Post Nat'l. Mon.
5
Dierks
L. GREESON
Murfreesboro
Crater of Diamonds S.P.
Arkadelphia
167
Rison
DeQueen
Nashville
Missouri
7
Fordyce
Star City
Cane Creek S.P.
Dumas
1
Old Washington Hist. S.P.
Prescott
7
Camden
Marks' Mills Battleground Hist. Mon.
Warren
Monticello
10
McGehee
Washington
MILLWOOD LAKE
Hope
White Oak Lake S.P.
Hampton
Dermott
Ashdown
Millwood S.P.
30
Poison Spring S.P.
Moro Bay S.P.
LAKE CHICOT
15
Lake Chicot S.P.
Texarkana
82
Logoly S.P.
Smackover
20
Arkansas Oil & Brine Museum
71
Lewisville
Magnolia
South Arkansas Arboretum
El Dorado
8
Hamburg
Lake Village
82
Conway Cemetery S.P.
167
7
82
Crossett
16
Wilmot
65

Legend

- ● State Park/Museum
- ◆ National Park/Historic Site/Monument
- ▲ Tourist Information Center
- ☼ Great River Road
- 〰 Lake/River/Creek/Bayou
- ⬡ Interstate Highway
- ⬡ U.S. Highway
- ○ State Highway

MILES 0 5 10 15 20 25
KILOMETERS 0 5 10 15 20 25 30 35 40

Arkansas Information

Please refer to the corresponding numbers on the map for the location of the following places mentioned in the book:

1. Beaver Lake
2. Blanchard Springs Caverns
3. Buffalo National River
4. Cooper Memorial Chapel
5. Cossatot River
6. Cossatot River State Park-Natural Area
7. Crowley's Ridge
8. Felsenthal National Wildlife Refuge
9. Grand Prairie
10. Great River Road
11. Hampson Museum State Park
12. Haw Creek
13. Hot Springs National Park
14. Highway 7 Scenic Byway
15. Lake Chicot
16. Lake Enterprise
17. Lake Ouachita
18. Little Maumelle River
19. Little Missouri River
20. Oil & Brine Museum State Park
21. Ouachita National Forest
22. Ozark Folk Center State Park
23. Ozark National Forest
24. Parkin Archeological State Park
25. Pinnacle Mountain State Park
26. Richland Creek Wilderness
27. St. Francis National Forest
28. Village Creek State Park
29. White River

For a free Vacation Planning Kit call
  800 NATURAL (628-8725) or
  800 644-4833 (V/TT)

Arkansas Department of Parks and Tourism
  501 682-7777 (V/TT)
  http://www.ono.com/arkansas
  74143.456@compuserve.com

Arkansas State Parks
  501 682-1191 (V/TT)

Arkansas Game and Fish Commission
  501 223-6351
  70550.2615@compuserve.com

Arkansas Highway and Transportation Department
  501 569-2227

Arkansas Industrial Development Commission
  501 682-7783
  http://www.aidc.state.ar.us.

Department of Arkansas Heritage
  501 324-9150
  501 324-9811 (TDD)
  http://www.heritage.state.ar.us
  info@dah.state.ar.us

U.S. Forest Service
  Ouachita National Forest- 501 321-5202
  Ozark-St. Francis National Forest - 501 968-2354

National Park Service
  Buffalo National River - 501 741-5443
  Hot Springs - 501 624-3383

Map (facing page) courtesy of the Arkansas Department of Parks and Tourism; computer-enhanced graphics by Patrick McKelvey, AdManInc.; relief detail provided by the Center for Advanced Spatial Technologies, University of Arkansas, Fayetteville

Gulpha Creek, Hot Springs National Park

Credits

One of the greatest joys in doing this book stemmed from working with the people involved.

Heartfelt thanks to all those who gave of their time to be photographed or quoted, and to the book's primary guiding forces—John Coghlan, Judy Wilbourn and Susan Bradley.

I would also like to express my gratitude to the following Arkansans who have helped with this project:

Sandy Alstadt	Jim Johnson
Collins Andrews	Bev Lindsey
Debi and Bill Barnes	Jo Luck
Don Barnes	Dayle McCune
Frank Barton	Jacqueline Cox-New
Steve Bova	Tom Orsini
Bill Bowen	Ron Payne
Helen Boyd	Mark Raines
Del Boyette	Joe David Rice
Sam Bracy	Kevin Sabin
Bennie Burkett	Bill Shepherd
Nancy Clark	Mary Gay Shipley
Ann Clements	Hallie Simmins
Richard Davies	Tom Steves
Nancy DeLamar	Kay Stebbins
Tim Ernst	Larry Stone
Mike Fitzpatrick	Randy Thurman
Jack Fleischauer, Jr.	Bruce Wesson
Jim Gaston	Randy Wilbourn
Tyler Hardeman	Amy Wilson
Bobbie Heffington	Townsend Wolfe
Russell Hoover	Shelby Woods
Mitch Jansonious	Sheila Yount
Curtis Jeffries	

Production Credits

Production Manager	John Coghlan
Text Editor	Judy Wilbourn
Photo Editors	Susan and Matt Bradley
Design	Matt Bradley
Typography	
Title	Creative Advantage Little Rock
Text	The Coghlan Group Fayetteville
Cartography	Max Gilbert
Prepress Color Proofing	Peerless Group of Graphic Services Little Rock
Custom Photographic Prints	Camera Mart Little Rock
Printing and Binding	Sung-In Printing Co., LTD Korea

State Hobie Championship, Grande Maumelle Sailing Club